A Parent Guide to Study Abroad

By
Stacie Nevadomski Berdan
William L. Gertz
Allan E. Goodman

New York

IIE publications can be purchased at: www.iie.org/publications

The Institute of International Education
809 United Nations Plaza, New York, NY 10017

Library of Congress Control Number: 2015938477

Managing Editor: Jon Grosh
Design: Pat Scully Design
Cover Concept: HDN Studios, Inc.

A Parent Guide to Study Abroad

Introductions

By Stacie Nevadomski Berdan

As parents, we all want what's best for our children. But "what's best" is not always clear. In today's interconnected world, one of the best gifts we can give our children is to help them develop a global mindset so that they will be best positioned for success in our competitive, global marketplace. But what does that entail, really?

Well, we must inspire our children to be curious about the world and to become globally aware. We must teach our children to communicate and interact with people across different cultures and in other countries so that they can begin to understand different points of view. We must do everything we can to help them begin to learn a second language as early as possible followed by the best opportunity to achieve language proficiency and cultural competency.

Studying abroad is one way to accomplish all of these things.

As parents, we have a significant impact on how our children view the world and whether or not study abroad is even an option. We should do everything we can to encourage our children to study abroad.

Studying abroad enhances global learning in that it requires our children to leave their comfort zone and encourages them to experience another culture and education system first hand. Studying abroad opens our children's eyes to new ways of thinking about the world. It helps our children learn to solve problems in cross-cultural contexts and supports critical thinking skills. Studying abroad is also one of the best ways for our children to acquire international experience, an increasingly important component to a college graduate's resume.

But all study abroad is not equal, thus making parental involvement in the process an imperative. Yet not every parent knows where to begin. For those who do, they may not know how to provide the right mixture of support as their child searches for the most affordable and appropriate program to meet their academic goals. That is why we wrote this book specifically for parents. It contains the critical information needed to be informed and to provide the best advice to our children as they navigate the entire study abroad experience.

Stacie Nevadomski Berdan
Author, Speaker, Global Consultant, Mother

By William L. Gertz

Like some of you, when I first went abroad many years ago, there was nothing to unplug.

I brought a backpack, four phrase books (German, French, Italian, and Spanish), a pocket knife, some clothes, and my harmonica. ATMs were not yet invented, so I cashed traveler checks at the exchanges. The convenience of cell phones did not exist, so needless to say, I never called home. There was no email, so I picked up letters at the American Express office in Paris. I traveled with my rail pass through 12 countries.

This three-month journey changed my life profoundly; I went away a boy and came back a confident and "worldly" man. When I returned to the United States, I began my career in international education, which became my life's work.

When my daughter went abroad during her junior year, I was excited for her. I wanted her to have "my" experience" (first mistake). But life is different nowadays, and you can't really unplug. While she was studying in Florence, we spent far too much time talking on Skype and communicating via Facebook. We were always connected; and while this was comforting for us both, it may have hampered the freedom she needed—the freedom of spirit, exploration, and trial and error that I had. Still, she came home a more confident, more accomplished young woman.

Her study abroad program was superbly organized down to every detail, perfect for the millennial generation, complete with ample hand holding. Days packed with detailed itineraries including learning excursions; volunteering trips and language courses were quite the contrast to my backpacking, hostel-hopping days of self discovery. Traveling by air on weekends, she probably had fewer adventures than I had traveling by rail. But I had to remember, this was her experience, not mine.

My strong advice is this: let your children breathe. Don't call too much, don't solve all their problems, let them make their own mistakes and find their own path.

As the song goes, "if you love someone, set them free."

William L. Gertz
President & Chief Executive Officer
American Institute For Foreign Study (AIFS)

By Allan E. Goodman

Bill and Stacie's introductions underline the important role parents can play and how best to perform it: have a plan and allow students to follow it without too much hand-holding or second-guessing, for there are many ways to study abroad and many ways to learn from the experience.

As parents, too, study abroad may prove to be the single most important ingredient to future success that you can help enable while your child is in college. A majority of the skills and emotional qualities needed to be successful in an intercultural workforce and global marketplace can be developed as a result of being on one's own in another country.

Most Americans still do not have that chance. The majority of U.S. undergraduates today are enrolled within 100 miles of their permanent home, and only about 10 percent study abroad. That is why the Institute has launched the Generation Study Abroad initiative to double that proportion and to reach this goal by the end of this decade.

When we announced this, one of our Trustees said we would not get there without also reaching out to parents to help them understand just how important international education is and how they can be supportive—hence this book.

It takes a village these days to do a lot of things in education. Parents are part of what makes education better in every community and at almost every level. But this may be the first time that we acknowledge just how critical their role may be in study abroad. With this in mind, we wrote this new book with a close eye to what would be most useful to a parent or close family member as you navigate how best to help and support your high school or college student in planning for an international experience as they map out their educational plans. We hope you will find this information to be of use.

Allan E. Goodman
President & Chief Executive Officer
Institute of International Education

CHAPTER 1

The Value of Study Abroad

Every student who hopes to succeed in the global economy should study abroad.

Globalization is everywhere, and it affects everyone in some way or another. Communications and technology have forever changed the way people interact by opening up borders for one-to-one communication without ever leaving home. Three factors—globalization, communication, and technology—have people around the world shifting to an increasingly borderless economy that includes politics, culture, and education. In order to give our children the best opportunity to succeed in this interconnected world, we need to provide them with opportunities to interact with the world beyond our borders.

Studying abroad offers students the competitive advantages and cross-cultural competence that open up a wealth of immediate personal and long-term professional opportunities. It can have a powerful impact on a young adult's life; most who've done so say it changed their lives. Yet only 10 percent of the approximately 2.6 million students who graduate with an associates or baccalaureate degree each year study abroad, which means relatively few are truly prepared to compete on a global scale. Our children depend on us to support and encourage them as they prepare to enter the workforce. If you want your child to succeed in today's competitive job market, do everything you can to help them study abroad and acquire international experience.

Studying abroad has evolved significantly over the years from what was commonly known as the junior year abroad studying language at a satellite university campus in a European city to diverse offerings for all undergraduate and graduate majors interested in study, volunteer, and internship opportunities for any length of time all over the world. With these many options comes a more complex decision-making process.

As a parent, you can champion study abroad as an essential component of your child's college education. You should encourage your son or daughter to begin thinking about studying abroad during his or her high school years and making studying abroad a part of the college selection process. All study abroad is not equal, and students should choose a college or university that fits all of their needs, including study abroad. Moreover, the sooner your child starts thinking about studying abroad, the more likely he or she will investigate options and stay true to his or her mission and not be blown off course by peer pressure on campus. Oftentimes students are short-sighted, peremptorily writing off study abroad as too expensive or deciding not to pursue it because of friends, a romantic partner, or sports or campus activities, not realizing—as we do as parents—that these reasons will probably fade in importance in only a few years.

The importance of international experience as a driver of career success, however, continues to move from a "nice-to-have" to a "must-have" criterion. Today's graduates need to develop a global mindset to succeed in the global economy. The study abroad experience plays a critical role in developing that global mindset, because it opens students' eyes to new ways of thinking about the world, instills a more informed approach to problem-solving in cross-cultural contexts, supports critical thinking in terms of considering multiple perspectives, and assists with open-ended, creative problem solving and reflection.

Studying abroad also enables today's students—future leaders from all backgrounds in all sectors—to acquire the international experiences that enable them to put their global learning into practice. Learning how to interact with people from other countries and cultures, including those in the United States, will be essential for all careers be they in business, manufacturing, engineering, government, academia, or not-for-profit.

The study abroad experience can help students to:

- Develop the global mindset needed to balance local and international challenges.

- Understand different cultures and solve problems while operating in a different environment.

- Open their eyes to other perspectives and ways of thinking about the world.

- Enhance their proficiency in and practical application of another language.

- Strengthen their adaptability, communication, and team-building skills.

- Increase their confidence, personal responsibility, and independence.

- Enhance their career opportunities.

STUDY ABROAD IMPROVES ACADEMIC PERFORMANCE AND GRADUATION RATES

In 2000, researchers began an ambitious effort to document the academic outcomes of study abroad across the 35 institutions in the University System of Georgia. The data included 283,000 students at 425 study abroad programs of all types (exchange/immersion, faculty-led, short-term, etc.) at research universities, and both two-year and four-year schools. Ten years later, they found that students who studied abroad had:

- Improved academic performance upon returning to their home campus;

- Higher graduation rates;

- Improved knowledge of cultural practices and context compared to students in control groups; and

- Benefited in their academic performance if they were students identified as "at risk."

The effects hold consistently across subgroups of gender, income, race, and SAT scores.

Documenting the Academic Impact of Study Abroad: Final Report of the GLOSSARI Project, by Richard C. Sutton and Donald L. Rubin, 2010.

What Value Does Study Abroad Offer Employers?

Tomorrow's college graduates are just as likely to work with people from as far away as Beijing and Bangalore as they are with those from Boston or Boise. Employers across all sectors increasingly seek workers with a combination of both technical and disciplinary skills as well as linguistic and cross-cultural competencies. Those who are best prepared for the new realities of the job market are the ones most likely to be hired first, and then to succeed. If your son or daughter is contemplating a career in international business, research, or diplomacy, global experience is a must. Regardless of his or her field, your child will benefit from having the soft skills—especially communication, analytical abilities, cross-cultural competence, and flexibility—that are the key benefits of studying abroad.

In research conducted for *A Student Guide to Study Abroad*, we interviewed dozens of professionals in multinational companies as well as global organizations about the value of study abroad. The vast majority responded that, if two applicants have essentially equal resumes, they would hire the one who had studied abroad, citing the following attributes:

- Cross-cultural awareness, which is critical to working on diverse teams;
- Ability to bring global thinking skills to bear on complex issues;
- Language skills needed in a multi-lingual world; and
- Predisposition to and experience with global mobility.

But, whereas study abroad in general might have been sufficient even a decade ago, the location your son or daughter chooses to study now is increasingly important in helping him or her stand out with employers. Eschewing traditional Western European countries in favor of China, Brazil, United Arab Emirates, South Africa, or India can signal an enhanced awareness of the growing global economy and helps young adults forge a direct link with the very places where many companies are expanding. While all countries provide valuable and marketable learning experiences, these nontraditional destinations often present more challenging situations for young Americans, which can intensify the learning curve.

In any case, just because your child studies abroad does not mean his or her potential employers will simply tick the box of international experience and hire them because of it. Overseas experience usually precipitates a whole line of questioning during the interview process, so your child must be prepared to discuss the value of his or her study abroad experience. Organizations will want to know what he or she did and learned and how he or she can bring that international experience to bear on the job. In order to reap the full benefits of study abroad, your child should therefore be immersed in the local culture as much as possible. By making local friends, living with a host family, and experiencing what it's like to live and study in a completely new environment, he or she can experience a different approach to teaching, learning, assignments, and homework. Working through these differences—and yes, making and learning from mistakes—will prepare your child to work with colleagues, supervisors, customers, and clients who come from different backgrounds.

After studying abroad, most students never view their education the same way again. They return home with a reinvigorated interest in academic pursuits and a renewed passion for learning. Studying abroad equips students with real-life, hands-on skills that no classroom can match.

CHAPTER 2

Investigating the Options

Studying abroad can be one of the most exciting experiences of your son or daughter's college career, but it is also a serious undertaking. It challenges students on a personal level. It will have an impact on his or her course of studies. It costs money. It's a big decision. As parents, you can help your child start thinking about study abroad in his or her freshman year (or better yet in high school) so as to have as much time as possible to consider the pros and cons, research the best options, and complete the application, which is often due months before departure. But the process takes time, and there is a great deal of information to consider for both you and your child.

Although your son or daughter will most likely have a study abroad office on campus that provides information, no one office or person has all the answers. There are simply too many different study abroad programs for one office to be aware of, much less know thoroughly. Encourage your child to start there, and offer to be involved in the process to help him or her make the best choice.

With that said, your degree of involvement will depend on your child. You may want to jump in and lead by the hand, but don't. Step back and let your child figure it out and take ownership. Consider it an opportunity for your child to become more independent and self-sufficient. Your son or daughter will need these skills while traveling in a foreign country without you. Conversely, you may feel as though you don't know how to help and want to remove yourself from the process entirely.

Don't. Your child will need your help as an experienced adult. Let your child take responsibility before and during the time abroad, but make sure he or she knows you are available for support and that there are key decisions that you need to be involved in.

Setting the Tone

As a parent, you have a significant impact on how your child views the world and, to some extent, whether he or she even considers studying abroad. Wherever you stand on the continuum of international experience—veteran world traveler or never been out of the country—the most important action you can take is to be supportive and informed, even if your child is handling everything. You may have some reservations about various aspects of study abroad. That's OK. Be sure, though, to take the time to investigate, gathering information and having discussions with your child about the ins and outs of study abroad. This shows that you are supportive, yet need more information. You can be your child's greatest advocate in pursuing study abroad and in preparing him or her for dealing with the fears he or she may experience as well as for the reactions from friends, family, and neighbors after expressing an interest in studying abroad. Conversely, you can also be your child's biggest obstacle.

Your child may be questioned as to why he or she is considering studying abroad. Despite being a nation of immigrants and now often described as a "tossed salad" more than a melting pot, as a whole Americans do not seem interested in what is going on in other countries or cultures, except perhaps from a heritage standpoint. In fact, Americans do not travel much outside the United States; less than half even have passports, many of which are military personnel, compared to 75 percent in the United Kingdom. Many people are afraid of going abroad; there is fear of the unknown and a discomfort with things that are strange and foreign. Some are afraid to leave family or are worried about interacting with people who have different religious beliefs, upbringings, and race and ethnicity. Regardless of the reason, not everyone agrees that studying abroad is a critical component to college education. Many people may even try to dissuade your child from going abroad.

If your child is on the fence about studying abroad, ask him or her the reasoning behind it. Most likely, one or more of the following factors are at play:

- **Media:** The daily news tends to focus on the rare disasters that happen to students abroad and the party-all-the-time attitudes of some instead of the links between study abroad experience and jobs. Share with your child the fact that millions of students have studied abroad without incident and that those that did occur were generally avoidable. Discuss with your child the importance of having fun, but also that this experience is about learning—not just partying and traveling. Find other parents who have children who have studied abroad, and discuss the experiences together.

- **Friends and family, including boyfriends or girlfriends:** Those staying behind often try to dissuade those contemplating studying abroad from doing so for a variety of reasons, particularly sports, romantic relationships, and campus social life. Encourage your child to share his or her rationale for going with naysayers, including the potential for experiences that will enhance his or her education. Be supportive as he or she emphasizes the reasons *to* go beyond the reasons *not* to go.

- **Language:** Do not let the fact that your child does not speak another language inhibit him or her from going abroad to a non-English speaking country. Although knowing another language certainly helps, it is not essential. His or her curiosity and willingness to learn about other cultures is more important. But encourage your child to study the host language before and after arriving, even if it is simply to order food and converse with local friends.

- **Fear:** If your child has not traveled outside the United States, he or she may be wary. You may be, too. Meeting new people can be nerve-wracking, and taking classes in a different academic structure may cause consternation about grades. You may worry that your child will be too far away to help if he or she has any sort of trouble. Show your child the short- and long-term importance of facing his or her fears and overcoming them.

- **Insufficient preparation:** Proper cross-cultural preparation is critical. Yet the vast majority of students do not receive it. The lack of intervention prior to, during, and after study abroad can inhibit your child's intercultural learning. Request that your child look into the type of preparation offered at various programs, and choose the ones that offer the cultural preparation that best satisfies his or her needs. Be persistent and ask for specific information, not just general advice.

THE WRONG REASONS TO STUDY ABROAD

If you think your child is looking for academic escape or a stress-free semester primarily spent gallivanting about, studying abroad may not be a good option. If your child simply wants to travel abroad, then encourage him or her to do so—and dispense with the studying part. Not only will it be less expensive overall, your child will be able to do it at the time of year that best suits his or her schedule and destination preferences, as not every destination will offer a suitable program. Just don't expect the same results. Studying abroad offers students an opportunity to take classes that are not offered on their home campus, often in a second language. Studying abroad offers the chance to combine studying a subject with real-life experiences. It enables students to study alongside students from the host country and a diverse group from around the world. Students abroad are in a learning environment, not just travel mode, which provides challenges—and rewards—on a completely different scale.

Most Common Types of Study Abroad Programs

No matter how large an undergraduate institution is and how many students it sends abroad every year, its menu of study abroad programs cannot possibly include the single best option for every student. As a result, institutions have developed a variety of different types of programs and partnerships, and it is important to understand the differences in order to make the most informed choice. Your child's study abroad office will provide information about the most common types of study abroad programs, each of which has pros and cons:

1. **University sponsored**: The college or university either owns its own overseas facilities or sends faculty members abroad to teach its study abroad students. The primary advantages of such programs are: the level of instruction is standardized (and known to the students beforehand), credits are guaranteed to transfer, and they are more likely to know their fellow participants. The downsides are that the professors will usually be from the home campus (with

fewer international perspectives) and that there will be fewer opportunities to meet other international students.

2. **Consortium:** The college or university works in conjunction with other academic institutions to form a single, collaborative program to which all partners have access, thus generally giving students a much wider range of approved programs from which to choose. However, since each school handles the process differently, any individual student's participation can be smooth or complicated, costly or inexpensive.

3. **Direct enroll:** Students enroll directly in an international institution, taking its courses and making their own travel arrangements. This can be done under the auspices of their university or independently. The greatest benefits of these programs tend to be the flexibility and independence involved, as well as the reduced cost. However, this generally means a greater time commitment (at least a full semester and often a whole year) on the student's part and considerable more research and preparation time before departure.

4. **Study Abroad Organizations:** An outside organization, such as the American Institute For Foreign Study (AIFS), the Council on International Educational Exchange (CIEE), and IES Abroad, make most arrangements, including submitting the application, organizing travel details, and arranging housing and excursions. This can be done under the auspices of a university or separately. These organizations, sometimes known as third-party providers, specialize in study abroad, and those that are well established tend to be very professional and adept at handling anything that arises. For students who haven't traveled much internationally before, and whose parents are inclined to worry, this is an attractive option.

5. **Exchange:** Exchange students swap places with a student from an overseas university through an arrangement between the two campuses. As there are generally only a certain number of participants and a limited number of exchange campuses, such programs tend to be highly competitive. It is, however, usually one of the least expensive options. Unfortunately, not all colleges offer exchange programs.

Once your son or daughter has discussed a variety of options with a study abroad adviser, he or she will most likely come away with stacks of information on many different programs. This would be a good time for you to discuss your child's academic goals and how various study abroad programs fit in with them.

Be a Sounding Board as Your Child Researches Options

Ask almost anyone who has studied abroad about their experience, and they will say it was a life-changing opportunity and one of the most rewarding things they have ever done. Ask these same individuals why they went, however, and the answers will be much more diverse. No matter the reasons for studying abroad, your child needs to depart ready and open to learning on an international level. In order to get the most out of the experience, your child should be focusing on the academic aspect of the program, not just the "abroad" part. Discuss a decision-making process with your child by asking this list of questions:

1. **What do you want to study while abroad?** Some students prefer to focus on their major, or a native language, or to meet diversification requirements in a creative way. And, of course, it could be a combination. Some students conduct research in the field or take part in an internship or service learning activity.

2. **How important is it that you earn credit?** In light of the often considerable financial outlay of studying abroad, the vast majority of students want to receive as much academic credit as possible for their time and effort. But not all need to receive a full term or semester's worth. So determine the minimum number of credits needed to stay on track for graduation or whether an experience matters more than a handful of credits.

3. **Where do you want to study and why?** Is there a specific country or region that interests your child, perhaps one that he or she might want to return to work and live in after graduation? Is there a specific language your child wants to learn? Is there a part of the world your child is exceptionally curious about and can't wait to begin exploring? The answers to these questions can effectively narrow the search for an appropriate study abroad program.

4. **Where and with whom do you want to live?** With a host family? In an apartment? In a dorm with other students? And if in a dorm, with other American students, with students from all over the world, or with local students?

5. **How long do you want to be abroad?** Options typically include anything from two weeks to a full academic year. Perhaps a January or May term, or a summer program. But remember, the longer the time spent abroad, the greater the learning experience.

6. **What role does language learning play?** Your child does not need to speak the language of a country to study there. It certainly helps, but the vast majority of programs cater to English-speaking students, meaning they can take classes in English. If, however, your child is proficient in another language, the benefits of taking classes in that language are great and should be pursued. Whatever your child's language level, he or she should make an attempt to learn the language in order to speak with locals, since that experience alone is of immense cultural benefit.

7. **What is the program going to cost?** While tuition, fees, and room and board account for the lion's share of the expenses of studying abroad, there are frequently other expenses involved, and students need to plan for these as well. Among the more obvious are airfare, visa fees, international health insurance, immunizations, and everyday expenses such as food and local transportation. But don't forget to account for additional expenses such as excursions, field trips, and mobile phones.

8. **Can scholarships or financial aid be applied?** Most can be for students participating in a university-approved program for credit, but your child must check with the study abroad office to make sure. If not, he or she will need to find an alternative source of funding.

9. **How will study abroad affect campus commitments such as a job, internship, or sports?** If your child has a job or internship, he or she should find out if time off can be granted and if it will be possible to resume upon return. If your child is involved in sports, investigate the possibility of a sports-training stint abroad, or perhaps consider a summer program.

10. **How much freedom do you want or need out of the experience?** Study abroad programs differ widely in their structure, formality, and level of independence. Keep in mind that there are pros and cons to all points on the spectrum and that living in another country offers a degree of independence all by itself.

11. **What do you want most out of the experience?** Ask your child to identify what he or she most wants to learn or experience so as to ensure that the study abroad program chosen will provide opportunities to achieve it.

12. **Do you have any special needs and can they be met?** Talk with the study abroad office and alumni with similar experiences. Be realistic about the challenges as well as open to the possibilities and opportunities. Research specific needs, build support networks, and trust in your adaptability and resilience once abroad.

This list should help you have a meaningful conversation with your child about the study abroad experience that is best for him or her and help you both begin to sort through the many considerations involved in selecting a program. The next best step for your child is to revisit the campus study abroad office and share these objectives with a counselor who can then begin identifying key programs and aligning them with your child's academic goals.

Aligning Education Goals With a Study Abroad Program

You may be skeptical about study abroad, as it has been criticized over the years for being an extended vacation or a lightweight academic term. Indeed, some programs are run more like glorified vacations, shuttling busloads of American students from one site to the next. Increasingly, however, these programs are the exception, not the norm. Yet the perception that study abroad isn't serious persists among parents, as well as others, such as professors and family friends, who may not understand the evolution that has taken place within the study abroad industry over the past few decades.

Compounding the problem may be your child's initial tendency to focus on the "abroad" part, a word that conjures up any number of romantic personal impressions or fantasies. There is no doubt that some students view studying abroad as a big vacation—and for those who do, a roundtrip ticket and a backpack are a whole lot cheaper than a structured study abroad program. But it is a serious undertaking, and you are advised to help your son or daughter understand that it is an opportunity to study, learn, and build valuable skills that will challenge your child on a personal level and have an impact on his or her academic and professional careers. Although studying abroad is great fun and invariably exciting, to be truly worthwhile it needs to also be academically and intellectually challenging. The best programs have solid reputations for academic rigor and cross-cultural outreach.

Too often, however, study abroad is considered an "add-on" and is not integrated within the undergraduate curriculum. To help ensure that your child gets the most out of his or her overseas experience, advise your child to investigate how best to integrate the abroad experience into his or her curriculum in order to maximize the international learning. Many programs now require language and academic preparation, research projects, presentations, or other rigorous academic work. Whether the program lasts three weeks or a full year, your child should begin with significant cultural and intellectual preparation well before leaving his or her home campus and conclude with an involved re-entry and reintegration course.

Encourage your child to seek out study abroad programs that offer academic rigor while providing a deep, cultural dive for the richest experience possible including:

- Pre-departure courses in history, geography, economics, and politics.

- Research assignments that require students to delve into a particular aspect of the destination country's history or culture and present their findings both before departure and again, with revisions, upon return.

- Inclusion of study abroad as part of a course, often business or international relations, by teaching from the perspective of a particular group, for example, customers, manufacturers, or government regulators.

- Intense language study, the goal of which is to reach a certain level of proficiency prior to departure.

- Interaction with international students on the home campus in order to help prepare him or her for cross-cultural interactions.

Once your child chooses a program, he or she will receive plenty of materials from the school, the host institution, and/or the program itself. There will be a great deal of information to absorb, so be sure to read all of the materials available and ask follow-up questions on everything from application deadlines and transportation upon arrival to class content and emergency plans. Sometimes students may not know which information to follow up on, so ask questions that your child can then ask the study abroad office or program provider. Moreover, the more you know about requirements, how the program works, the host country, and opportunities and challenges, the more assured you will be and the more supportive you will be able to be. Don't hesitate to ask other parents for advice, and double check facts related to visas, safety, and health on U.S. government websites. Although you may have some reservations about your child studying so far away from home, your support is critical for his or her success. Encourage your child to go, learn a lot, and have fun!

ENCOURAGE LANGUAGE STUDY

One of the most practical and immediate benefits of studying abroad is language acquisition. Therefore, encourage your son or daughter to consider programs that provide an opportunity to study another language, especially in an immersive or semi-immersive manner. In addition to the cultural insights that your child will gain, language skills are becoming an increasingly important differentiator among hiring managers. Even if your child is not proficient, a solid working knowledge of another language indicates an openness to—and appreciation for—other cultures, a critical 21st century skill. And if your child hasn't studied language much at all, encourage him or her to start learning on campus or through any one of the free online programs before going abroad and to be a dedicated learner on the ground.

When it comes to language destinations, encourage your son or daughter to keep an open mind. French speakers are not limited to France; French is also spoken in Belgium, Canada, Côte d'Ivoire, Guinea, Senegal, and Switzerland, among others. If your child is learning Spanish, Spain certainly fits the bill, but so, too, do Argentina, Chile, Costa Rica, Mexico, and Peru, just to name a few. These countries also have the added benefit of being part of Latin America, an increasingly important region to the United States on many fronts.

CHAPTER 3

Figuring Out the Financials: Cost Models, Financial Aid, and Scholarships

Although study abroad certainly isn't cheap, it doesn't have to be cost-prohibitive either. The cost of studying abroad varies greatly depending on the type and location of the program, the length of stay, and whether the program is administered through a university or an outside agency. While the overall cost of studying abroad often exceeds that of studying on the home campus—which may lead students to consider it unaffordable—it is a mistake to make this assumption beforehand or to assume that the difference is prohibitively large. Some study abroad programs can actually be less expensive than tuition and fees for the equivalent amount of time on the home campus. Encourage your son or daughter to research financial aid, scholarships, and grants, and compare costs associated with location, time-frame, and type of program. The earlier your child starts, the more options he or she will have to compare. It is imperative, however, that your child begin at his or her own study abroad office and then keep them informed throughout the process, even if your child ends up pursuing outside opportunities.

Program Cost Models

The cost of a study abroad program is a summation of several factors. First and foremost is the cost of the program itself, which varies based on the type of program— a university-run program, a university-affiliated program offered through a study abroad organization, or an unaffiliated program—and its length. Services such as local staff support, orientation or language training programs, social activities, and excursions all affect the price of the program.

Compare Programs

Many colleges and universities are committed to maintaining cost parity, meaning a semester abroad costs exactly the same as one on the home campus, at least as far as tuition and board, for programs offered by the university. Some institutions even reduce the price of the credit hour for study abroad programs. Generally speaking, these programs will typically break the cost down into three categories: what students pay to the home university, what students pay to the host institution, and estimates of additional costs. University-sponsored or university-affiliated programs will most likely charge the regular semester tuition, a study-abroad fee, and trip and/or medical insurance. The cheapest option, therefore, is usually to enroll directly at a local university or college and take its courses and make your own travel arrangements. This can be done under the auspices of the college or independently, but know that it requires significantly more time commitment and independence on your child's part than university-led programs. Your child will need to manage almost everything, from confirming student visas before departure to making sure transcripts are sent and accepted upon completion.

Housing and Food

Housing is usually an additional expense charged by the host university. But the cost will vary depending on where your child chooses to stay—with dorms, apartments, hostels, and homestays being the standard options. Homestays in particular can significantly reduce the cost of living and offer the added benefit of immersion in a local family setting.

What and how your child eats also affects costs. Preparing his or her own food in a dorm or kitchen, buying food in local markets, and eating out sparingly—lunches are generally cheaper than dinners—will reduce costs.

Location

Location can also make a big difference in price. Western European countries such as England, Italy, and Spain are inherently more expensive than developing countries such as Peru, Senegal, or Thailand. The difference has to do with the host country's overall standard of living and the overall cost of basic goods and services. Your child should research the cost of living among target countries by looking up exchange rates, the Consumer Price Index, and cost of living statistics. Some of the more helpful websites are **Expatistan.com**, **Numbeo.com**, and **Databank.world.org**. If your child is interested in a popular destination, there may be many different types of programs offered by different organizations. As a result, prices should vary, often significantly.

Length of Stay

Naturally, the length of stay also has an impact on price, with longer programs typically costing more. However, there can be exceptions, most notably when a student enrolls in a foreign university for a year, or even a semester, and pays significantly less than his or her home campus tuition. Moreover, some students have spent less money over the course of their college career by taking more courses that are less expensive overseas, oftentimes enabling them to graduate in less than four years. Students who follow this path usually must withdraw from their home university and apply to another, negating any and all fees and costs associated with their home university. Taking this approach can save your child (and you) a great deal of money, but it is not without risks. Take care to ensure that all credits can be transferred and that all official paperwork is collected and copied, with back-up copies kept in a safe place.

Additional Expenses

There will be a variety of additional expenses such as airfare, meals, books and school supplies, visa and passport, immunizations, excursions, travel within and outside of the country, international insurance, and spending money based on the program and the student. Before even choosing a program, it is imperative that your son or daughter knows exactly what is included in the cost of the program and what is not. Study abroad offices can provide this information—as can the offices of nonaffiliated programs—but advise your child to read the fine print and be sure to ask about the cost of elements not included. Your child should do online research and contact program coordinators to ask for specific information.

Determine if Financial Aid Can Be Applied to Study Abroad

Any financial aid that your child is already receiving from the university should be transferable to a study abroad experience run by or affiliated with that university, since the tuition that you will be paying to study abroad probably goes directly to your home university. Some institutions will also allow students to use their student aid for nonaffiliated programs, while others will not. Moreover, the amount of aid may vary depending on the type of program they choose. Just don't assume that whatever aid your child is currently receiving from his or her school will transfer over; he or she needs to check with the financial aid office.

Federal financial aid can be applied to any program as long as credit is earned and the home institution accepts the transferred credits. Simply have your child fill out the Free Application for Federal Student Aid (FAFSA). If your child is already receiving federal aid, he or she is usually not required to reapply. The same goes for state funding; it varies from school to school, so be sure to check.

Private Scholarships

Private scholarships differ in their rules regarding studying abroad, so your son or daughter may or may not be able to apply these scholarships to a study abroad program. Advise your child not to assume and to confirm the situation with the scholarship provider sooner rather than later.

Research Study Abroad Scholarships

Every year, tens of millions of dollars in scholarships are given to U.S. students to study abroad. Most universities with study abroad offices have a wealth of information about the various kinds of scholarships offered by a variety of sources.

Regardless of where your child wants to go or what he or she wants to study and for how long, encourage him or her to look into all the study abroad–related scholarships and grants available as soon as possible, even beginning as a freshman. Students must apply for scholarships, and some can be very competitive.

Generally speaking, there are five types of study abroad scholarships:

- **Merit-based:** These awards are based on a student's academic, artistic, athletic, or other abilities, and often factor in the applicant's extracurricular activities and community service record.

- **Student-specific:** These scholarships are primarily awarded to individuals who meet certain demographic criteria, typically based on gender, race, religion, family background, or economic status. Scholarships for minority students are the most common.

- **Destination-specific:** These are scholarships awarded by a particular country to students planning to pursue a study abroad program in that country. They are awarded as an incentive to study in that country rather than somewhere else.

- **Program-specific:** These scholarships are offered to qualified applicants by individual study abroad programs and/or the colleges and universities that sponsor them. These scholarships are often given on the basis of academic and personal achievement, but qualifications do vary.

- **Subject-specific:** These scholarships are awarded by study abroad programs or institutions to students based on their major or field of study. These scholarships often require the recipient to enroll in subject-specific courses or conduct subject-specific research while abroad.

Most colleges have a straightforward framework for applying for study abroad scholarships, one that lays out the potential amounts available, the process and deadlines for applying, and any restrictions that may exist. General scholarships for study abroad assistance as well as targeted scholarships for underrepresented and first-generation students and students with high financial need are usually offered.

U.S. Government-Sponsored Scholarships and Fellowships

Benjamin A. Gilman International Scholarship Program
This program, sponsored by the U.S. Department of State's Bureau of Educational and Cultural Affairs, provides scholarships to American undergraduates of limited financial means to pursue international exchange programs, including study abroad, international internships, and service-learning, from four weeks to one academic year for academic credit. **www.iie.org/gilman**

> *Studyabroadfunding.org offers detailed descriptions of hundreds of study abroad scholarships, fellowships, grants, and career-oriented internships for U.S. undergraduate, graduate, and post-graduate students, as well as professionals.*

Fulbright U.S. Student Program
Established by Congress in 1946 and sponsored by the U.S. Department of State's Bureau of Educational and Cultural Affairs, the Fulbright Program supports educational exchanges that strengthen mutual understanding between the United States and more than 140 participating countries for one academic year. It is a partnership program in which the U.S. and foreign governments jointly set priorities. **www.fulbrightonline.org**

Critical Language Scholarships for Intensive Summer Institutes
A program of the U.S. Department of State's Bureau of Educational and Cultural Affairs, the Critical Language Scholarship (CLS) offers fully funded, group-based intensive language instruction and structured cultural enrichment experiences abroad for seven to ten weeks for U.S. citizen undergraduate, master's, and PhD students in thirteen critical needs languages: Arabic, Azerbaijani, Bangla, Chinese, Hindi, Indonesian, Japanese, Korean, Persian, Punjabi, Russian, Turkish, and Urdu. **www.clscholarship.org**

Boren Awards for International Study
The David L. Boren Scholarships and Fellowships, sponsored by the National Security Education Program, provide funding opportunities for U.S. undergraduate and graduate students to study in world regions critical to U.S. interests and underrepresented in study abroad. Boren Scholars and Fellows represent a variety of academic backgrounds, but all are interested in studying less commonly taught languages. Boren Awards promote long-term linguistic and cultural immersion, and thus the majority of recipients study overseas for at least six months. In exchange for funding, recipients commit to pursuing employment with the federal government. **www.borenawards.org**

Funding Offered by Private Organizations
Funding is also available from foundations and other sources that support international study and research. A few examples include:

- AIFS Scholarships

- CIEE Grants and Scholarships

- Rotary Foundation Scholarships

- Whitaker International Fellows and Scholars Program

Scholarships Offered by Foreign Governments or Organizations
Foreign governments and private organizations also can be a great source of funding for your child's study abroad program. A few examples include:

- German Academic Exchange Service (DAAD)

- Chinese Government Scholarship Program

- French Embassy Benjamin Franklin Travel Grant

- US-Japan Bridging Foundation

CROWDFUNDING

Students have been fundraising for causes for decades, but social media has enabled them to move beyond washing cars and selling candy door-to-door to tap into a global network of potential resources through crowdfunding. Students choose a crowdfunding site, post their pitch — their program, dates, and the purpose of the funds such as airfare, course costs, visa fees — as well as upload a photo or video, and promote the link to family and friends. Kickstarter, IndieGoGo, and Fund My Travel are some of the most popular.

Ways to Save Money on the Ground

Although program costs are fixed, there are many ways to save money on the ground, depending on where your son or daughter is studying:

- Open a local bank account.
- Buy a local SIM card or possibly a cheap local phone.
- Ask for student discounts.
- Bargain, haggle, and negotiate.
- Use Skype or other free online services to communicate back home.
- Live like a local.
- Be smart about transportation, biking or walking most places.
- Be a thrifty traveler.
- Set a budget and track expenses.

Listen to Those Who Know

As a parent, you should make a point of talking with other parents who have children who have studied abroad, and you should encourage your child to do the same with other students on campus. Someone who has been to the location recently will be able to tell you how much things really cost and how much he or she spent above and beyond the "posted" price of the program. Advice specific to the country your child is visiting or the currency he or she will be using will be especially helpful. But don't just accept everything you are told. Each person's experiences will be unique, and not everyone's advice will apply to your child.

Studying abroad can be affordable. The vast majority of costs are going to be predetermined before your child departs, but there are plenty of ways to save money on the ground. Doing research and working with the study abroad office will be critical to success. It is up to your child to sort through the information and select a cost-effective program. Either way, it is a great investment in your child's future.

CHAPTER 4

Staying Safe and Healthy While Abroad

While the benefits of studying abroad are immense, the thought of one's child living in another country can rattle the nerves of even the most easygoing parents. Rest assured that the odds of your child's having a safe and incident-free study abroad experience are in your favor, regardless of where your child goes. Indeed a majority report feeling safer abroad than they do in the United States.

Still, there are inherent risks in traveling, studying, and living abroad, and your son or daughter needs to be prepared for them. It is important to remember that there are bad actors everywhere and that there is no such thing as a completely safe destination, be it abroad or here in the United States. And while some criminals do prey specifically on tourists and students, the vast majority of problems students have while studying abroad are either minor (such as petty theft or minor illness) or self-inflicted (such as drinking too much or financial crisis brought on by poor money management). Even if your child feels completely comfortable with the inherent risks, they must still think about personal safety. Common sense and good judgment are the best tips for staying safe anywhere in the world, so one of the most important things you can do for your child is to make sure he or she is mature enough to study abroad and that he or she approaches the experience seriously.

Research the Risks

Crime knows no borders; it takes place around the world. Natural disasters can strike anywhere, and their effects can be exacerbated by the inferior infrastructure found in poorer countries. Political unrest can break out and suddenly cut students off from friends and family back home. While you may not approve of your child's studying in a place that is perceived or even documented to be dangerous or unhealthy, it is important to check the facts. For example, crime and disease statistics are almost always given for the overall population—not the small subset of tourists or international students that your son or daughter will be among. Some of the best sources of truly helpful information are:

● The U.S. Department of State, which issues country-specific travel advisories and up-to-date information on health and safety issues, especially in those countries where extra caution is warranted. The site also offers safe travel tips—a comprehensive list of action steps to take both before departing and while traveling.

● The Centers for Disease Control and Prevention (CDC), which provides detailed information on staying healthy while traveling, including—but not limited to—lists of required immunizations and other health recommendations, tips on food and water safety, and confirmed outbreaks of disease.

● Travel guides, books, and websites focused on living abroad offer valuable health and safety information, not only about countries or cites in general, but also about specific locations.

Be Informed

One of the best ways for your child to stay safe is to be as informed about his or her destination as possible before arriving. Encourage your child to seek out information from official websites such as those listed above, as well as from fellow students who have studied abroad there. Students who have been there will not only be encouraging and supportive, they will be able to offer practical, relevant, and recent information. Here are a few other tips to suggest to your child:

● Research current events, customs and culture, politics, economics, history, religion, geography, and climate.

- Read about the everyday behaviors and practices of the people well before departure and from several different sources.

- Talk to people who either grew up in or spent considerable time in the country where they are going and ask them specifically about differences in social behavior to be aware of.

- Ask about U.S. stereotypes people may have encountered while studying abroad and how to deal with them.

- Read evaluations written by students who have studied abroad in the host country.

Talk About Health and Safety

Whether your child is a seasoned traveler or a first-timer, he or she must think about personal safety and understand the risks inherent in being a stranger in a foreign land. A little bit of planning and a lot of awareness on the ground can go a long way in keeping your child safe. In addition to your child doing research on his or her destination, you should talk together about the importance of staying safe and healthy in an unfamiliar environment. Advise your child to:

- **Be especially alert upon arrival.** A combination of fatigue and excitement may blind your child to the dangers that may be lying in wait upon arrival. Have a prearranged plan to leave the airport or train station.

- **Be familiar with local laws.** Once on foreign soil, your child is subject to that country's laws. He or she should know the local laws, follow them, and pay attention to what's going on by reading the local newspaper and asking friends and campus advisers any questions they may have.

- **Get to know the neighborhood.** Become familiar with the new surroundings as quickly and conveniently as possible.

- **Avoid carrying important or valuable items.** His or her passport (and other valuables) should remain in a safe, locked place, though your child should carry a photocopy of the passport whenever he or she goes out. Keeping small amounts of cash in more than one place, such as a wallet or purse and tucking a few small bills into a pocket for easy reach are wise practices.

- **Stay fit and healthy.** Encourage your child to make healthy food choices, exercise, drink moderately, stay hydrated, and get plenty of sleep.

- **Be careful on the roads.** Advise your child not to rent a car unless he or she has to, avoid taxis without seatbelts, and only take buses from an established and recommended company, opting for the safest route rather than the fastest.

- **Be aware of cultural norms.** Encourage your child to become familiar with the local cultural standards, respect them, and be ready to reflect those standards in their own actions where appropriate.

- **Guard against pickpockets and petty theft.** Teach your child to be aware of his or her surroundings while out and to be wary of anyone asking for help or offering currency exchange or tour services.

- **Develop a contingency plan for everything from lost luggage to emergency evacuation.** Your child will be less likely to panic when confronted with a problem if he or she already has some idea of the best steps to take.

Encourage Common Sense

No matter how well your child knows the local language and his or her way around, plain-old common sense will play a key role in staying safe.

- **Protect valuables.** Encourage your child to leave anything valuable home when going out, including his or her passport, unless the situation requires it. A passport photocopy, however, should be carried at all times, saved as a photo on his or her phone, and saved in an email. Your child should also email himself or herself important information, such as credit card numbers and bank accounts, to retrieve should they be lost or stolen. Encourage your child to use a money belt and carry small bills in readily accessible places for quick purchases.

- **Be smart with money.** Teach your child to manage his or her money, to know what things cost, not to wave money around, and to stick to a budget.

- **Keep family or friends apprised of his or her whereabouts, especially when traveling.** If other people know generally where your child is and his or her expected arrival times, they can sound the alarm in a timely manner.

- **Maintain a low profile.** Clothes, mannerisms, language, and especially guidebooks and maps will make your child stand out as a nonnative. By blending in, your child is less likely to be singled out as a potential target of crime.

- **Don't walk around at night alone.** Your child may feel safe and the city or country may be safe, but why court trouble? No place, after all, is safer at night than it is during broad daylight. And there is always more safety in numbers, especially if your child gets lost or encounters difficulties.

- **Don't take shortcuts, back alleys, or poorly lit streets.** Even if your son or daughter is in a hurry, it is better to be late than waylaid. Stick with wide, well-traveled streets that are well lit and well known.

- **Don't accept food or drinks from strangers.** If your child starts to feel strange or intoxicated, he or she should immediately alert a friend or an official such as a police officer. Since there will be no way of knowing the cause of his or her symptoms, your child may need to go to the hospital.

- **Don't get drunk.** It's only natural that your child will want to party with his or her new friends. Tell your child to go easy and stay in control.

- **Don't use drugs.** If drugs are illegal, don't use them—period—even if your child is already familiar with them and their effect. For starters, some countries' laws are extremely strict, and there may be no way to plea bargain out of being caught with them by saying "I'm not from here". In addition, they may be adulterated or of poor quality. And even where drugs are legal, stay away and stay in control.

- **Practice safe sex.** Travel prepared with condoms, and don't take risks.

- **Don't get cornered.** Your child, if with someone he or she doesn't know well, should avoid certain situations and locations, such as a car, an apartment, or a deserted beach or park.

- **Stay away from high-crime areas.** If your child is aware that certain parts of town are unsavory, he or she should stay away from them. If your child really must go there, a trusted local friend should come along and only during daylight hours.

- **Be aware of anti-American sentiment.** There is little that can be done about pervasive or persistent anti-Americanism. But your child can downplay being conspicuously American and try to look like he or she could be from any number of Western nations. Register with the STEP program on the U.S. State Department's website, and use the buddy system.

- **Pay attention to the news.** What you don't know can hurt you, so your child should keep up with local events. For example, a transportation workers' strike might leave him or her stuck somewhere. Imminent elections may spark political demonstrations. Or there may be a fresh rash of robberies on certain modes of public transportation in certain areas.

- **Look out for scams.** Unfortunately, travelers of all types have fallen victim to any number of scams designed to get them to part with their money. Your child should be wary of giving or lending people money, and watch out for any bargain that looks too good to be true—it probably is!

Advice for Women Abroad

It is an unfortunate and unfair fact of life, but women must be more careful than men when it comes to staying safe abroad. And this means not taking chances, even ones that they might feel perfectly justified taking at home. Growing up in the United States has given your child a perspective on gender roles that may be significantly different from those of your child's host country. In addition, most cultures will have impressions of "what American women are like"—impressions acquired mostly through movies and television shows. We all know how unrealistic those tend to be, but the foreigners who view them may not. So your child—specifically your daughter—needs to know what those perceptions are and be prepared to encounter them. The most pernicious of these, and the one that they need to be most on guard against, is that American women are "easy."

Unfortunately, a woman can find herself enforcing that stereotype without even meaning to by the way she smiles, makes eye contact, strikes up conversations, or just consorts with male students. This is because cultural norms can be deceptively different. What may signify absolutely nothing to an American may speak volumes to foreigners, especially those from restrictive cultures. It is important

WILL MY CHILD BE TREATED UNFAIRLY WHILE ABROAD?

Each student's experience is different, but regardless of race, religion, gender, physical disability, or sexual orientation, it is possible that your child may face discrimination abroad. The possibility is the same as on your child's home campus or even hometown. While most students have had positive experiences abroad, the following tips can help you prepare to deal with discrimination while abroad.

Tips for Dealing With Discrimination While Abroad

- **Do your homework together.** The best way to deal with discrimination abroad is to prepare yourselves by learning about the historical and cultural dynamics of the host country. This can provide clues about what to expect while abroad. Working with your child to identify current news outlets, blogs, or other online resources can help you keep up with the current cultural issues of the country.

- **Ask around.** If your child believes he or she has experienced discrimination, advise your child to explain the situation to someone he or she trusts from the host country, such as the program staff or host family. It's important to get a local perspective before making assumptions about the meaning of those particular actions. Many parts of the world are not as diverse as we are in the United States, so being different may incite genuine curiosity, such as staring or touching, though these actions are not done with malicious intent.

- **Report it.** If your child is harmed in anyway, he or she should report the incident to the program staff immediately. They should be able to direct your child to the nearest legal authorities. Make sure everything has been documented, so the details can be reported thoroughly. While racism and discrimination do not receive the same legal treatment in other countries as they do in the United States, reporting the incident allows your program directors to address the issue to the best of their abilities.

Special contribution from *Diversity Abroad*

to remember that local people will view your child through their cultural lenses. And for women especially, misinterpretations can have unpleasant and even dangerous consequences.

Your daughter should therefore respect the culture of her host country by dressing and behaving appropriately. It's best to err on the conservative side until she completely understands local norms. Here are a few tips for staying safe as a woman while abroad:

- Be aware that in many countries, women do not have equal rights.
- Don't be caught by surprise; be aware of your surroundings at all times.
- Err on the side of caution when it comes to strangers.
- Carry cash in a discreet place.
- Dress conservatively, especially at night and when it's hot outside.
- Don't plan to arrive late at night or alone at an unfamiliar place.
- Always use the front entrance to your hostel or apartment.
- Don't walk alone at night unless it is absolutely necessary.
- Use common sense and put safety first.

Emergencies

In the event of an adverse situation affecting U.S. citizens, the local U.S. embassy will post notices on its website, broadcast information through local media channels, and contact U.S. citizens using any known email addresses or phone numbers or via the STEP program if your child has registered, as they should have (see Page 40). In the rare case that the situation is potentially life threatening, the embassy will advise all U.S. citizens to leave the country, and it may be able to offer some assistance in doing so. If your child is studying in or traveling to a country that is prone to natural disasters, such as volcanic eruptions or floods, or places where political and social upheaval is commonplace, he or she should take extra precautions by becoming familiar with evacuation plans on the country's website. In most cases, your child—or his or her program—will need to arrange for commercial transportation.

Medical Treatment

Medical practices vary widely throughout the world, and it is important that you and your child understand the basic healthcare system of his or her host country. Your son or daughter can always check in with the local U.S. embassy or consulate to inquire about recommended doctors, clinics, or hospitals.

If your child takes the proper health and safety precautions before leaving the United States and does his or her best to stay healthy, odds are he or she will have an incident-free experience abroad.

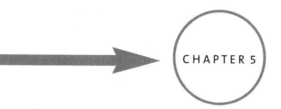

CHAPTER 5

Preparing Your Child for Success Abroad

Once your child has chosen a program, there is still much to do before departure, and waiting until the last minute is always a big mistake. In addition to making sure your child completes the application on time, applies for or renews a passport, and secures any necessary visas, he or she needs to start considering the intellectual, emotional, and physical aspects of the upcoming study abroad experience.

Preparing, though, is more than just buying a ticket, selecting courses, and saying goodbye to friends and family. Relocating to another country, under any circumstances and for any length of time, is a serious undertaking. Your child must take initiative to research the country, culture, and people in order to gain the knowledge and information necessary to have a successful study abroad experience. You may be helping a great deal or simply kept "informed." Make sure you know what you need to know and what your child needs to do well before departure.

Help Your Child Get Organized

Once your child has selected a program, made sure that he or she meets any and all eligibility requirements, and confirmed that the program matches his or her personal and academic objectives, an application must be submitted, generally before a fixed deadline. Once your child has been admitted, acceptance paperwork, including a legally binding contract and course selections, must be completed. Be sure to read the entire contract carefully with your child, especially payment and refund policies.

Travel Arrangements

If your child is going abroad with his or her college or any U.S.-based program, outbound travel arrangements will probably be taken care of by the sponsoring institution, though your child may have a few options to select such as departure city and carrier. If your child needs to make his or her own arrangements, however, make sure they are made as soon as possible, particularly if traveling during peak seasons. Regardless of whether your child is buying his or her own ticket or going with a group, inquire about the possibility of leaving the return open, so that your child has the option of staying on afterward to travel. In any case, the return trip should always be scheduled a few days after final exams to allow time to pack and complete any administrative or physical obligations, such as cleaning out a dorm room or apartment.

If your child is not being met at the airport, make sure he or she has a workable plan for leaving the airport in order to reach the final in-country destination. You should also agree on how and when your child will contact you upon arrival.

Passport

You will want to be sure that your child has a valid passport and, depending on where he or she is going, a visa. Most countries require that a passport be valid for at least six months beyond the date of a return ticket; if not, it must be renewed. Both getting a new passport and renewing an old one are a lot easier than most people think, but it takes time, money, and the acquisition of certain documents, most notably an authorized copy of a birth certificate. For detailed instructions and information, go to the U.S. Department of State's website on passports. Note: parents should have a valid passport as well, in case an emergency trip is needed.

Visa

A visa is an official stamp, seal, or document affixed in a passport that allows entry into another country for a specified amount of time and for a specific purpose. A visa is required for a stay longer than 90 days in most countries, and some countries require students to have a study visa regardless of the length of time. U.S. citizens can determine if they need a visa by visiting the website of the country or by going to the U.S. Department of State's website and clicking on "Country Specific

Information." If a student requires a visa before departure—and your program should inform your child if it is (but always double check the information)—the student is responsible for obtaining it. He or she will need to know where to apply, what materials are required, and when to apply. Depending on the country and access to a consulate or embassy, the application process may take anywhere between a week and a few months and can sometimes be a protracted process. It is very important to consider the timeline for applying for a visa and to submit the application as soon as possible.

Depending on your child's destination, his or her program adviser may advise the student to *not* apply for a visa prior to leaving the United States, but to extend his or her visa once in country before the 90 days expires. Carefully verify this advice with the U.S. Department of State's website. If your child does not have the necessary visa, he or she may be denied boarding the plane, or denied entry upon arrival in country. Visa rules can change, and it is up to your son or daughter to make sure he or she has the most up-to-date information.

Healthcare

Before departure your child should have a general physical and arrange for any required or recommended vaccinations. Any pending dental work should also be done before going abroad. Make sure he or she packs a complete medical record, any prescription medications, and an extra pair of glasses, if applicable. Even if your child will have other coverage while studying abroad (many study abroad programs require it), continue carrying your child as a dependent on your health insurance policy. Be aware that in many countries the patient must pay the cost of medical services in advance, or treatment is denied. The Centers for Disease Control (CDC) website offers comprehensive health and medical information for travelers on required immunizations, staying safe in country, and what to do if travelers become ill or injured.

Important Information and Documents

Encourage your child to make several copies of important documents. Have him or her leave a copy of each document with a trusted family member or friend at home and scan and save them to his or her hard drive or upload them to a secure location to allow digital access. Important documents include passport, visa (if applicable), credit or debit cards (both the number and the contact information), and emergency contact information on the ground in the host country: the 911 equivalent, the U.S. embassy or consulate, and emergency services for both home and host institutions.

U.S. STATE DEPARTMENT'S SMART TRAVELER ENROLLMENT PROGRAM (STEP)

Two to three weeks before your child leaves, have him or her register for the Smart Traveler Enrollment Program (STEP) on the U.S. State Department website. It is easy to do; travelers fill in their name, destination, length of stay, and how they can be reached overseas. The State Department will use this information to send important security or emergency messages, whenever warranted. These could include safety alerts (strikes, civil disturbances, protests), health warnings (disease outbreaks), and significant changes in bilateral relations. If your child plans on traveling beyond the host country, simply update the STEP profile to reflect new dates and destinations. You and your child can download the free "Smart Traveler" app at the State Department website.

Help Your Child Create a Workable Financial Plan

Once your child has chosen a study abroad program and decided how to pay for it, the next step is to determine how much money will be needed for incidentals such as airfare, visa, healthcare, and living expenses. The first three need to be assessed and planned prior to departure, and each will have a known cost. The last, living expenses, is much less predictable. The country's cost of living plays a large role in determining how much your son or daughter will end up paying for housing, meals, transportation, and other day-to-day expenses. It will also affect the amount of spending money your child will need to bring and manage.

For starters, he or she should look at the exchange rate, compare the cost of living between the host country and the United States, and ask other students who have gone before for advice. Sometimes students fall into the trap of spending more money than they realize because the currency is different.

Create a Budget

Next, create a budget with your child in the currency of the host country. Identify the expense categories and set a budget for each, or create a master budget for the entire time, and set a daily allowance. Whichever your child uses is personal preference, but in either case, he or she will need to track expenses and monitor spending on an ongoing basis. If your child begins to go over budget, advise him or her to put the brakes on spending until the budget can be readjusted, which should be done immediately. Busting their budget is perhaps the easiest way that students can get into trouble overseas, and one that will quickly compromise the enjoyment and hence value of the study abroad experience.

Accessing Money

Decide how to access money for both everyday financial needs and in the case of emergencies. One of the most cost-effective ways to manage money in another country is to open a local bank account. If that is not feasible, have your son or daughter ask his or her bank if its ATM card will function abroad and what extra fees are involved, and inform the bank before leaving of the impending travel so it doesn't suspect fraud and freeze the account. Discuss the pros and cons of withdrawing large and small sums of cash; larger amounts minimize transaction fees, but entail greater consequences in case of loss or theft. Consider the option of bringing credit cards or preloaded debit cards—those that require showing a passport—with money that can be added by a family member back home. Although both are safer than carrying cash, using them may incur fees, and they may not be accepted often enough to be worthwhile.

Spending and Saving Money

Have a conversation with your child about ways to save money on the ground. As noted in Chapter 3, some tips include buying food in local markets as opposed to eating in restaurants, taking public transportation instead of taxis and walking or riding a bike as often as possible; asking about student discounts (and carrying a student ID with them at all times); using Skype to stay in touch with family and friends; finding the best mobile phone option or if he or she needs to bring it at all; using cash whenever possible, and bargaining whenever appropriate.

USING MOBILE PHONES ABROAD

Mobile phones are common all over the world and are helpful during emergencies and communicating with local friends. Explore all options to determine which phone will work best for your child based on the amount of time abroad, the location, and his or her budget. Most U.S. cellular providers offer supplemental services and plans for overseas usage, but some may be quite expensive or require mobile phones that are incompatible with foreign networks. Your child may also buy a local SIM card for his or her U.S. phone, though the card will only work in an unlocked tri-band or quad-band phone. Another option, probably the most popular and cost-efficient for students staying a semester or more, is to buy a local cell phone (and SIM card) upon arrival. Former students and/or program organizers can provide details on the best local stores and service plans.

Help Your Child to Think Globally

As a parent, you can also help your child prepare for the intellectual, social, and psychological experience by encouraging him or her to develop a global mindset. Developing a global mindset means thinking globally about schoolwork, friends, the foods they eat, the news they read, the clubs they join, communication and interaction with people who are different, and their future. In essence, students should consider studying abroad as an opportunity to open their minds to the world and its people, places, ideas, and events. Research the host country with your son or daughter both to demonstrate interest and become informed. Encourage your child to prepare for the cross-cultural exchanges by enhancing his or her global persona before, during, and after studying abroad by:

- Paying attention to world events and international news.

- Monitoring global political trends.

- Cultivating listening skills and other personal skills that enhance cross-cultural interaction.

- Learning or practicing a second language.

- Following national news online for the relevant country and region.

- Joining local and virtual international clubs.

- Making friends with international students on the home campus.

- Paying attention to issues around the world they care about.

PACKING

When it comes to packing, it may be best for you, as a parent, to minimize your involvement. Your child will probably be given packing recommendations from the school or program and probably knows the basics of what he or she needs and can live without, or buy upon arrival. If you want to prevent big packing blunders, offer your child this general advice:

- Make a checklist so as to not forget anything.

- Pack only what you can carry (one medium suitcase with wheels, one large backpack, one daypack/carry-on).

- Don't pack valuables in checked luggage.

- Attach sturdy ID tags to luggage, plus a colorful ribbon or tie for easy visual identification.

- Check the airline's baggage policy and weight limitations.

Encourage Your Child to Seek Out Cross-Cultural Training

One of the benefits of studying abroad is acquiring cross-cultural competency. To do so requires first understanding the many differences between one's own culture and the new culture one is entering. Some differences are clear and obvious, others subtle and much less so. Culture constitutes the cornerstone of our identities—who we think we are, the ways we make meaning, and what is important to us and why. Cultural differences are a key source of conflict between people.

Cultural differences can and often do interfere with communication and interpersonal relationships. Evidence collected over several decades by anthropologists and cross-cultural experts shows that most people would benefit from some sort of preparation and training before crossing cultures. Exposure to short introductory information sessions alone may not be enough to prepare your child for the different environment he or she will encounter overseas. Failure to prepare properly can prevent your child from getting the most out of his or her investment. Good training programs can help students better adapt to new environments by giving them a specific framework to:

● Understand differences between/among cultures.

● Learn cross-cultural communication dos and don'ts.

● Develop skills to adapt to new environments.

● Work within diverse teams.

● Provide an overview of the cultural, historical, political, and economic fundamentals of the host country.

Of course one-size does *not* fit all, and training can never cover every situation. But good preparation will help your child develop problem-solving techniques that can help him or her excel academically and live and work successfully across cultures.

Unfortunately, the vast majority students who study abroad do not get proper cross-cultural training. Encourage your child to seek out cross-cultural training on campus and, if it is not thorough enough, have them check out "What's Up with Culture," a free, online cross-cultural training program developed by the University of the Pacific. Your child can also read up on cultural differences in the *Culture Shock!* series or Xenophobe's Guides available in bookstores, in libraries, and online.

Give Your Child Practical and Sentimental Gifts

Your child is going on an adventure and, as such, you and other family members may feel compelled to give them a gift. If your child is like most students, the gift of cash is usually the most appreciated, but also consider giving both practical and sentimental gifts for the journey. Some ideas include:

- A **passport holder** with zippered pockets to keep travel documents safe and organized.

- A **multi-day backpack** that is small enough to carry on a plane, but large enough to fit items for 2-3 days; it should be waterproof and have multiple pockets both inside and out.

- A **Swiss Army-type knife** with a sharp blade and multiple tools yet small enough to fit in a pocket. (Note: Knives must be stored in checked luggage when flying or they will be confiscated.)

- A **universal power adapter** because electrical outlets vary by country and region and are often incompatible with U.S. equipment.

- **Books/Literature** are great travel companions and should be specific to a destination such as travel or culture guides, literature or fiction, or history or other nonfiction, all either digital or paperback.

- A **journal** to log thoughts, impressions, emotions, and hesitations that is not too fancy to draw attention but perhaps includes a few special photos or hand-written sentiments by you.

- **Creature comforts of home:** Sentimental gifts from home will be appreciated, such as a hand-written packet of letters to be opened once a month; a family picture set in a light, unbreakable frame; or a small care package of favorite foods or candies to be savored when the taste of home is most desired. Depending on the length of your child's stay, you may want to send such gifts along after your child arrives; just be aware of the timeframe involved and the cost of shipping packages.

Another practical gift is *A Student Guide to Study Abroad,* a comprehensive, practical "how to" book filled with information and offered in a fun and engaging style. All aspects of study abroad are covered in detail including what students should do before they go, while abroad, and when they return. This hands-on resource includes 100 easy-to-follow tips and dozens of real-life stories. Each chapter features useful quotes and anecdotes from a diverse collection of students, advisers, and professionals.

Reassure Your Child

As the date of departure nears, your child may begin to doubt himself or herself and express concerns and fear. He or she may even contemplate backing out. This is completely normal; traveling overseas, saying goodbye to family and friends, and managing numerous details, big and small, can be overwhelming. Don't dismiss these reactions as silly; they are real and your child needs to hear that you have confidence in him or her and his or her ability to handle this big adventure. Your child has grown a lot since arriving as a freshman. Tell your child that you are confident he or she is capable of handling whatever might arise during his or her time abroad, and that if not, there are resources available.

As a parent, you should be involved on at least two levels. One, be sure to ask your child if he or she has covered all the important steps noted in this chapter and ask for copies of any and all relevant travel documents, especially flight information and host contact information. Two, you should encourage your child to have the right attitude—that he or she is going abroad to learn, experience, and be immersed in another culture.

CHAPTER 6

Supporting Your Child While He or She Is Abroad

Once your child has left, it is time for you to let go and be supportive from afar. Succeeding abroad depends largely on your child's ability to effectively adapt to the local culture, which is not always easy. Your child needs to pay attention to what is going on, notice things big and small, and fall into the local rhythm. He or she will need to make new friends and acquaintances and get to know his or her new neighborhood. Things will be strange and new, so it is best if your child takes it all in, discusses it with others on the ground, and begins to adapt on his or her own. This adaptation process is one of the areas of growth for most students.

In order to truly experience another culture, experts recommend complete immersion—language, living arrangements, food, activities, and more. To be sure, most first-time study abroad participants are not ready for this deep dive, and you should not expect them to be. But you should encourage—and help—your child to immerse himself or herself as much as possible, even if on a university-led program. To do so, your child must break from home and the home culture as much as possible. This generally translates into infrequent calls, and limiting consumption of social media and American music and movies.

Culture Shock

As a parent, it is important to understand culture shock, because your child is going to experience it in some way, and you will need to educate yourself on its three phases so you are not caught off guard when it happens. Technically speaking, culture shock is the confusion, disorientation, and emotional upheaval that come from immersion in a new culture. Culture shock typically follows a three-phased cycle starting with a honeymoon period in which everything feels grand. But fabulous turns to frustration, depression, and confusion and is often triggered by an event involving seemingly minor cultural differences or misunderstandings. All usually ends well, however, as the recovery phase restores equilibrium after one has regained confidence and learned to appreciate the new culture as a whole.

Stay in Touch—But Not Too Much

Although staying in contact is easier than ever these days with the availability of mobile phones, Skype, email, and texting apps, be prepared to have less frequent communication with your child than usual. You may want to hear how things are going, and your child probably wants to share, but remember that if your child is constantly checking in with you and his or her friends at home, he or she may not be taking the time to make new friends and local contacts. Moreover, the less your child checks in with you, the more independent he or she becomes. In order to get off to a great start, speak to your child once or twice upon arrival. But then set up a regular form of contact that gives you both peace of mind but is not obsessive, perhaps one email per week and a Skype every few weeks or once a month. Remember, less frequent communication does not mean lower quality communication.

When you do interact, listen more than talk. Give updates on family news, but don't overload or overwhelm your child to the point of making him or her homesick. Be positive and supportive, even if you miss your child, so that he or she does not begin to feel guilty. Ask questions about what your child has seen and done, but also what has surprised him or her and what has not. Encourage your child to share photos periodically. Make sure your child knows you are glad he or she has taken this important step and that you can't wait to hear all about the experience and the great stories once they return home.

Limit Use of Distracting Technology

Current communication technologies enable students to stay connected to U.S. culture, which is generally not a good thing. Encourage your child to minimize use of social media, as well as American music, movies, and to some extent, books. Some people argue that these comforts from home soothe anxiety and help a student settle in better. But feeling disconnected, isolated, lonely, and, yes, even temporarily overwhelmed are an important part of the study abroad experience. If your child chooses to study abroad, then help him or her do so by leaving all but the most essential technological and cultural trappings of American life behind.

Don't Get Too Involved

Adjusting to a new environment is not easy for anyone, and almost everyone who spends significant time abroad experiences some degree of culture shock. Since part of the study abroad experience is learning how to overcome difficulties and move past them, students must figure it out for themselves. It can be frustrating, though, and your child may even go through a phase of negativity, discouragement, and homesickness where nothing is right or good. You will be tempted to try to solve the problem—and may even consider flying there to console him or her. Don't, unless your child is in serious trouble. Listening may be one of the most important, and undervalued, communication skills that we use. Be sure to keep an open mind and reserve judgments. This doesn't mean you shouldn't ask questions if you are alarmed or concerned—by all means do so—but don't rush to judgment, because you may not have all the relevant information. Show support and understanding during the difficulty, but avoid getting too involved. Encourage your child to first make use of the student support services that are available or their local contact and be sure to ask if things are improving or working out. Your child will be much happier and more confident knowing that he or she was able to overcome difficulties independently, both upon returning to the United States as they go through similar experiences, and for the rest of his or her life.

Offer Tips for Making the Most of the Experience

You want your child to thrive during his or her study abroad experience, not just survive, so offer him or her some strategies for making the most of the experience. Every student comes back with a slightly different story of how they grew emotionally, intellectually, and cross-culturally. Few say it was easy, but your child can learn from those who have gone before. When you speak with your child, encourage him or her to:

- Get to know people and make local friends.

- Be a tourist, explore and see the sights.

- Try something new every few days.

- Find sports or clubs of interest and participate.

- Learn and practice the language.

- Adapt to the local culture.

- Don't blame locals for problems.

- Learn from mistakes.

Visit With Discretion—or Not At All

Visiting your child while he or she is abroad will provide you with a great opportunity to share in his or her cultural experience. Keep in mind, though, that students abroad are not on vacation; they are there to learn and attend class. They will have homework, projects, and deadlines. They will also be developing their own lifestyle. Take care not to interrupt any of these aspects of your child's time abroad. Don't plan on attending class with your child or taking him or her on sightseeing trips unless it is at the end of the semester or term. In fact, the best time to visit is at the very end of the program, during a semester break, or during a scheduled vacation so that you can travel together. This will enable your child to be your host in their temporary home, showing off how to get around like a local, eat in popular, local restaurants, and see sites off the traditional tourist path. Be sure to do your homework before you visit so that you are sensitive to local customs and cultural norms in the host country lest you embarrass your child.

It may be difficult, but once your child is on his or her way, you must let go. Your child has taken all the steps necessary to having a successful study abroad experience. Show excitement and support for your child as he or she shares funny stories, tells tales of woe, and sends photos of amazing sites and new friends. There will be plenty of time later to ask the hundreds of questions you have. Write them down—even consider keeping a journal—and be prepared to listen to your child once he or she returns home, transformed by the experience.

CHAPTER 7

Helping Your Child Transition Back Home

Your child is coming home. Whether it has only been a few weeks or a whole year, the time probably flew by for both of you. If your son or daughter is like most other students, he or she will probably feel a combination of excitement and nervousness: excitement because he or she is coming home to see family and friends and to catch up on all the things he or she has missed. But also nervous about reintegrating with old friends, readjusting to life on a U.S. campus, and missing the independent, international lifestyle they have been living. As a parent, it is essential that you try to understand the wide range of feelings your son or daughter is likely to experience. Your child has changed, probably a great deal. Some things may be obvious, others subtle. Take the time to listen and get reacquainted, acknowledging that you may not be able to help him or her adjust. You can, however, advise your child on ways to incorporate the study abroad experience into the rest of his or her time on campus and eventually in the job market.

Prepare for Transformation

Most study abroad students report years later that the time they spent abroad in college changed them for life. How widespread and deep those changes will be depend on your child, how comfortable he or she felt abroad, and how long and deep the cultural immersion was. It may be confined to a few superficial tastes or mannerisms, or it may cut to the core of his or her beliefs. But one way or another, your child's head will be forever screwed on differently. This can be difficult for you as a parent to adjust to. To be sure, each student's experience is going to be unique, but some of the ways that your child probably will have changed are by having:

- A greater sense of independence,

- Better communication skills,

- An enhanced ability to build relationships,

- Increased adaptability,

- A greater acceptance of diversity,

- More patience,

- Improved diplomatic skills,

- Strengthened or reinforced core values, and

- A strong desire to go abroad again.

And because your child has changed, so too will his or her relationships with others, including you. This can be a difficult for both of you, so be supportive, and again, listen to your child. He or she may have a difficult time at first articulating what he or she is experiencing, and you should allow time to work through it. Readjusting will require both time and the same skills and approach he or she used while abroad, because the experience will be reverse culture shock.

Understand That Reverse Culture Shock is Real

Experts agree that reverse culture shock is actually more difficult to get through than traditional outbound culture shock. With reverse culture shock, your child feels out of place in his or her own country, and that sensation is generally more fundamentally disorienting than feeling out of place abroad, where you are, in fact, somewhat out of place. As with traditional culture shock noted in Chapter 6, your child will experience the same three phases: fabulous turns to frustration, which returns to normal in the recovery phase. Recovery takes places as your child finds his or her new niche and learns how to integrate his or her study abroad experience into post-experience life.

Your child's program and/or university may have ways of helping returning students deal with reverse culture shock, but don't rely solely on them. Encourage your child to seek out ways to deal with it on his or her own. As a parent, you may not be able to help your child through the process directly, but you can help indirectly by encouraging him or her to:

- **Share stories.** The better able your child is to tell a good story about his or her time abroad—stories that capture the experience in a simple, engaging, yet dynamic way—the better he or she will be able to connect with an audience, be they friends, other family members, roommates, or potential employers. Encourage your child to think through how he or she has changed and what it means on a personal and intellectual level.

- **Talk with people who have had similar experiences.** Your son or daughter will want to keep in touch with friends made abroad in order to relive some of the shared experiences and reconnect with that special time. He or she can also seek out others on campus, or through friends, who have also recently returned to talk about what they went through, how they are adjusting, and how "home" is now different. Empathetic ears go a long way toward resolving reverse culture shock.

- **Seek out authentic international culture at home.** Your child has lived in another culture for weeks, if not months, and will probably be yearning for aspects of the culture, such as food, music, language, or people. Help connect your child with local elements of that culture. Enjoy it with them, too!

- **Continue language learning.** If one of your child's reasons for studying abroad was to learn or enhance second language skills, don't allow all the progress he or she has made atrophy. Languages need to be used and practiced daily to keep it up, which is generally easily done via campus clubs or classes, online conversation clubs or apps, international students or immigrant neighborhoods, or culture (movies, books, music).

- **Document memories.** Your child probably has many photos and all kinds of mementos from his or her time abroad. Help him or her find the most meaningful way to capture the overall experience—perhaps a digital photo book, a video story, a blog, or even a large poster of photos, tickets, and quotes. Your child will benefit more by having reminders of the experience handy as opposed to leaving them in the proverbial shoebox stuffed under a bed or in a closet that rarely sees the light of day.

- **Keep thinking globally.** Your child may be frustrated with other peoples' lack of interest in things global, be disillusioned with the United States, and develop a strong desire to go abroad again. Encourage your child to find how best to make the study abroad experience become part of his or her new self and to begin blending this experience with the next chapter in his or her life.

- **Share the experience on campus and at his or her former high school.** Your child can help students who are considering going abroad by serving as a role model and peer counselor. Back on campus, he or she can volunteer as a past participant at orientations; back home, he or she can make a special visit to his or her former high school. Having a college student return and speak to high school juniors and seniors can be a powerful motivator.

Building on Global Experience Both On Campus and Off

Once your child has returned, the experience is partially over (for now). But learning and growing can and should continue. First and foremost, your child should build on his or her burgeoning "global citizen" persona by continuing to develop global awareness and cross-cultural competency. This means continuing to explore and experiment with new or expanded academic and personal interests, tastes, styles, and ideas. Encourage your son or daughter to take advantage of available opportunities—on campus and off—to incorporate more international experiences and resources into his or her life. Not only will your child learn and have new and enriching experiences, he or she will prove to prospective employers that his or her term abroad was not just another college course to be put aside once the final exam is over, but the beginning of a long and personal independent study program. A few examples of how your child can engage are:

- Affiliate with global groups on campus.

- Reach out to community organizations.

- Enjoy global food, music, movies, and art.

- Continue to seek out international friends.

- Travel abroad on a personal vacation.

Leveraging the Study Abroad Experience

Your child is now a member of a small group of students—less than 10 percent—that has international experience prior to graduating. This experience constitutes a real marketplace differentiator. Yet one of the biggest mistakes that students who have studied abroad make when it comes time to apply for jobs is not incorporating all of their global learning into their job-search materials. All too often it is listed as one line at the bottom of a resume rather than leveraged as an asset. Whether your child is interested in a global job or not, the study abroad experience can be a useful and powerful tool. Global experience matters in today's job market more than it ever has before.

Identify Lessons Learned and Skills Developed

In order to fully leverage his or her study abroad experience, your child will need to be able to articulate his or her growth. So many students return from studying abroad asserting emphatically that "It was the best time of my life!" But they cannot express why it was or how they changed. Immediately following your child's return, advise him or her to articulate exactly how he or she has changed, with a special emphasis on identifying skills acquired that may help in the job search and be relevant to longer-term career pursuits.

Incorporate Study Abroad Into Job-Search Materials

Employers are looking for graduates with international skills, and study abroad experience is one of the best ways to showcase a global mindset. Encourage your child to highlight his or her cross-cultural competence in his or her resume, cover letter, and job interview. In preparation for job interviews, your child can reference his or her travel journal and reflect on previous conversations with you about his or her growth and learning.

With respect to his or her resume, your child should be sure to include both cross-cultural aptitudes and international skills. This can be presented in at least two ways. First, include a descriptive sentence or two about the study abroad experience, including, where, when, and what he or she studied, learned, or gained from it. Second, infuse the resume with the "soft skills" associated with cross-cultural competence, such as flexibility, communication, relationship-building, and curiosity. And if your child studied a language abroad, be sure to draw prominent attention to that as well.

In preparation for a job interview, have your child practice answering the question: "Tell me about your study abroad experience." Again, the answer should not be, "It was the best time of my life!" but rather to provide a thoughtful response as to why he or she went, what he or she learned, and how these new skills can be applied to the job in question. Also remind your child to practice incorporating some of the lessons learned while studying abroad into answers for interview questions.

Networking is an important aspect of any job search. Encourage your son or daughter to maintain the relationships they made while abroad, and begin to make new connections now that he or she is back in the United States. You never know where some of these contacts might eventually lead.

Now that your child has tasted what it is like to live abroad, he or she may want to do so again. Some students take a gap year upon graduating from college to travel, volunteer, or teach English abroad; many pursue graduate studies abroad; and others join global service organizations such as the Peace Corps. Encourage your child to pursue the avenues he or she is most passionate about. With globalization at our doorstep, the more international experience your child has, the better prepared he or she will be to not only compete in the global economy, but to solve global problems through international dialogue and collaboration.

Author Biographies

Stacie Nevadomski Berdan | Stacie Nevadomski Berdan is a seasoned global executive, an expert on international careers, and an award-winning author on how to succeed in the global marketplace. She spent the majority of her career at Burson-Marsteller and Unilever, where she served as strategist, coach and counselor to CEOs, politicians and senior executives around the world. Her extensive global leadership experience in corporate communications and marketing, public affairs, organizational communication, and cross-cultural consulting extends across four continents with a specific focus on Asia.

Stacie uses her international business experience to promote the need for global awareness and cross-cultural competency for all in her books, media appearances, bylined contributions, and speaking engagements across the country. Her recent book, *Raising Global Children*, is a combination parenting-advocacy book that was the first of its kind to detail what raising global children means, why global awareness is critical, and how to develop a global mindset in children today. Her first two books, *Go Global! Launching an International Career Here or Abroad* and *Get Ahead By Going Abroad: A Woman's Guide to Fast-Track Career Success*, are the go-to guides for global careers. Her numerous broadcast media appearances include NBC's "Today Show," NPR's "Marketplace," ABC News, CNN and FOX, and her work has been featured in *The New York Times*, *Wall Street Journal*, *USA Today*, *Chronicle of Higher Education*, *Huffington Post*, *Forbes* and *Time*. **stacieberdan.com**

William L. Gertz | Since 2005, William L. Gertz has served as President and CEO of the American Institute For Foreign Study (AIFS), a leading organization in the field of cultural and educational exchange. With more than 30 years of experience in International Education, Mr. Gertz has led many initiatives that have been instrumental to the growth and direction of the company including leading it to its most successful years to date. Today, AIFS College Study Abroad sends 5000 students to over 20 countries around the world every year. Total annual worldwide participants on AIFS educational programs, including Au Pair in America, Camp America, Academic Year in America, Summer Institute for the Gifted, Cultural Insurance Services International, American Council for International Studies, and College Study Abroad, are approximately 40,000. Under his leadership, AIFS was voted the fourth best place to work in Connecticut for mid-sized companies by Workplace Dynamics and Hearst Newspapers. Mr. Gertz is the Vice Chairman of the AIFS Board of Directors and is a Trustee on the AIFS Foundation Board.

In addition to his role as AIFS President and CEO, Mr. Gertz has published numerous articles in educational publications including the *IIENetworker* magazine and *Youth Travel International*. He is also active in the field of gifted education serving as a Trustee for the National Society for the Gifted and Talented, a non-profit organization, and previously serving on the State of Connecticut Board of Gifted and Talented Students. Mr. Gertz was also a member of the Development Committee for NAFSA: Association of International Educators and is currently a member of the Board of Directors for the Alliance for International Educational & Cultural Exchange. In 2010, Mr. Gertz organized the Diversity in International Education workshop in Washington, DC, and in May of 2014, he received an Honorary Doctorate in International Relations from Richmond, the American International University in London.

Allan E. Goodman | Dr. Allan E. Goodman is the sixth president of the Institute of International Education (IIE), the leading not-for-profit organization in the field of international educational exchange and development training. IIE conducts research on international academic mobility and administers 250 corporate, government and privately sponsored scholarship and training programs. Previously, Dr. Goodman was executive dean of the School of Foreign Service and professor at Georgetown University. He is the author of books on international affairs published by Harvard, Princeton and Yale University presses.

Dr. Goodman was the first American professor to lecture at the Foreign Affairs College of Beijing, helped create the first U.S. academic exchange program with the Moscow Diplomatic Academy for the Association of Professional Schools of International Affairs, and developed the diplomatic training program of the Foreign Ministry of Vietnam. He is a member of the Council on Foreign Relations, a founding member of the World Innovation Summit for Education (WISE), co-president of the Partner University Fund (PUF) Grant Review Committee, and a member of the Thomas R. Pickering Foreign Affairs Fellowship Program and the Jefferson Scholarship selection panels. Dr. Goodman has a Ph.D. in Government from Harvard, an MPA from the John F. Kennedy School of Government and a BS from Northwestern University, and numerous honorary degrees as well as the Légion d'honneur from France. He was awarded the inaugural Gilbert Medal for Internationalization by Universitas 21 in May 2012.

About the Publishers

Institute of International Education (IIE) | The Institute of International Education is a world leader in the exchange of people and ideas founded in 1919. IIE has a network of 18 offices worldwide and 1,400 college and university members. In collaboration with governments, corporate and private foundations, and other sponsors, IIE designs and implements programs of study and training for students, educators, young professionals, and trainees from all sectors with funding from government and private sources. These programs include the Fulbright and Humphrey Fellowships and the Gilman Scholarships, administered for the U.S. Department of State, and the Boren Scholarships and Fellowships administered for the National Security Education Program. IIE also provides advising and counseling on international education, and conducts policy research. IIE's publications include the *Open Doors Report on International Educational Exchange*, supported by the Bureau of Educational and Cultural Affairs of the U.S. Department of State, as well as *Funding for United States Study*, print and online versions of *IIEPassport: The Complete Guide to Study Abroad Programs*, and the StudyAbroadFunding.org website. **www.iie.org**

American Institute For Foreign Study (AIFS) | Founded in 1964, the American Institute For Foreign Study is one of the largest and most experienced cultural exchange organizations in the world. With global offices in five countries, AIFS organizes cultural exchange programs for more than 30,000 participants each year. AIFS programs include college study abroad, au pair placement, international camp staffing, gifted education, high school study/travel and insurance services. More than one and a half million students and teachers have participated in AIFS programs worldwide. AIFS awards more than $600,000 in scholarships and grants each year. In affiliation with 23 universities in 19 countries, the AIFS College Division organizes study abroad programs annual for more than 5,000 American students during the semester, academic year, summer, and January term. AIFS works closely with more than 500 American colleges and universities, providing students and faculty with high-quality educational experiences abroad. **www.aifs.com**

The American Institute For Foreign Study (AIFS) Foundation, an independent, not-for-profit, 501(c)(3) tax-exempt public charity, was established in 1967 with the assistance of the late Senator Robert Kennedy to help young people from many nations and diverse cultures to better understand one another. The AIFS Foundation provides grants to high schools, individuals and institutions to encourage international and educational travel. The AIFS Foundation also sponsors the Academic Year in America (AYA) program, which enables more than 1,000 international teenage students to spend a semester or academic year with an American host family while attending the local high school. **www.aifsfoundation.org**

IIE Web Resources

GENERATION STUDY ABROAD™
Generation Study Abroad is a five-year IIE initiative to double the number of U.S. college students studying abroad by the end of the decade. IIE actively seeks new partners and resources to achieve this goal.

WEBSITE: www.generationstudyabroad.org

IIEPASSPORT.ORG
This free online search engine lists nearly 10,000 study abroad programs worldwide and provides advisers with hands-on tools to counsel students and promote study abroad.

WEBSITE: www.iiepassport.org

STUDY ABROAD FUNDING
This valuable funding resource helps U.S. students find funding for study abroad programs.

WEBSITE: www.studyabroadfunding.org

FUNDING FOR UNITED STATES STUDY
This directory offers the most relevant data on hundreds of fellowships, grants, paid internships, and scholarships for study in the United States.

WEBSITE: www.fundingusstudy.org

INTENSIVE ENGLISH USA
Comprehensive reference with more than 500 accredited English language programs in the United States.

WEBSITE: www.intensiveenglishusa.org

BENJAMIN A. GILMAN INTERNATIONAL SCHOLARSHIP PROGRAM
The Gilman Scholarship supports U.S. undergraduates of high financial need at two-year or four-year colleges or universities in the United States to study or intern abroad for academic credit. Awards are granted for fall, spring, and academic year terms of up to $5,000, or $8,000 for students studying a critical need language.

SPONSOR: U.S. Department of State, Bureau of Educational and Cultural Affairs
WEBSITE: www.iie.org/gilman

BOREN SCHOLARSHIPS AND FELLOWSHIPS
Funding supports U.S. undergraduate and graduate students to study less commonly taught languages in regions critical to U.S. interests: Africa, Asia, Central and Eastern Europe, Eurasia, Latin America, and the Middle East. Up to $20,000 is awarded to undergraduates and $30,000 to graduate students. Recipients commit to work in the federal government for at least one year after graduation.

SPONSOR: National Security Education Program (NSEP)
WEBSITE: www.borenawards.org

Programs of the AIFS Foundation

The AIFS Foundation

The mission of the AIFS Foundation is to provide educational and cultural exchange opportunities to foster greater understanding among the people of the world. It seeks to fulfill this mission by organizing high-quality educational opportunities for students and providing grants to individuals and schools for participation in culturally enriching educational programs.

WEBSITE: www.aifsfoundation.org

ACADEMIC YEAR IN AMERICA (AYA)

Each year, AYA brings nearly 1,000 high school students from around the world to the United States. They come for the school year to live with American families and attend local high schools, learning about American culture and sharing their own languages and customs with their host families.

WEBSITE: www.academicyear.org

FUTURE LEADERS EXCHANGE PROGRAM (FLEX)

Established in 1992 under the FREEDOM Support Act and administered by the U.S. Department of State's Bureau of Educational and Cultural Affairs, FLEX encourages long-lasting peace and mutual understanding between the United States and the countries of Eurasia.

YOUTH EXCHANGE AND STUDY PROGRAM (YES)

Since 2002, this U.S. Department of State high school exchange program has enabled students from predominantly Muslim countries to learn about American society and values, acquire leadership skills, and help educate Americans about their countries and cultures.

Programs of the American Institute For Foreign Study

American Institute For Foreign Study

The AIFS mission is to enrich the lives of young people throughout the world by providing them with educational and cultural exchange programs of the highest possible quality.
WEBSITE: www.aifs.com

AIFS COLLEGE STUDY ABROAD

AIFS is a leading provider of study abroad programs for college students. Students can study abroad for a summer, semester, or academic year in 17 countries around the world. Faculty-led and customized programs are also offered.
WEBSITE: www.aifsabroad.com

AMERICAN COUNCIL FOR INTERNATIONAL STUDIES (ACIS)

For more than 30 years, ACIS has helped students and their teachers discover the world through premier travel and education. Teachers can choose destinations throughout Europe, the Americas, and Asia.
WEBSITE: www.acis.com

AU PAIR IN AMERICA

Au Pair in America makes it possible for nearly 4,000 eager and skilled young adults from around the world to join American families and help care for their children during a mutually rewarding, yearlong cultural exchange experience.
WEBSITE: www.aupairinamerica.com

CAMP AMERICA

Each summer, Camp America brings nearly 6,000 young people from around the world to the United States to work as camp counselors and camp staff.
WEBSITE: www.campamerica.aifs.com

CULTURAL INSURANCE SERVICES INTERNATIONAL (CISI)

CISI is the leading provider of study abroad and international student insurance coverage. Since 1992, CISI has insured more than 1 million international students and cultural exchange participants worldwide.
WEBSITE: www.culturalinsurance.com

SUMMER INSTITUTE FOR THE GIFTED (SIG)

SIG is a three-week academic, recreational, and social summer program for gifted and talented students. Students from around the world in grades 4 through 11 can participate in SIG Residential programs offered at university campuses across the country including Bryn Mawr College, Emory University, Princeton University, UC Berkeley, UCLA, University of Chicago, University of Miami, Vassar College, and Yale University. Day, part-time, on-line and Saturday programs are also offered. SIG operates under the National Society for the Gifted and the Talented (NSGT), which is a nonprofit 501(c)3 organization.

WEBSITE: www.giftedstudy.org

AIFS Information and Resources

The following resources are available for download at www.aifsabroad.com/advisors/publications.asp

- Student Guide to Study Abroad and Career Development
- Diversity in International Education Summary Report
- The Gender Gap in Post-Secondary Study Abroad: Understanding and Marketing to Male Students
- Study Abroad: A 21st Century Perspective, Vol I
- Study Abroad: A 21st Century Perspective, Vol II: The Changing Landscape
- Innocents at Home Redux—The Continuing Challenge to America's Future
- Impact on Education Abroad on Career Development, Vol. I
- Impact on Education Abroad on Career Development: Four Community College Case Studies, Vol. II

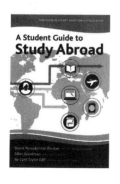

A Parent Guide to Study Abroad is a companion to the comprehensive *A Student Guide to Study Abroad*, which is a hands-on resource with 100 easy-to-follow tips and dozens of real-life stories. Each chapter features useful quotes and anecdotes from a diverse collection of students, advisers, and professionals. Like the parent guide, *A Student Guide to Study Abroad* covers all aspects of study abroad including what students should do before they go, while abroad, and when they return. Both guides are available at **www.iie.org/publications** (bulk discounts available).